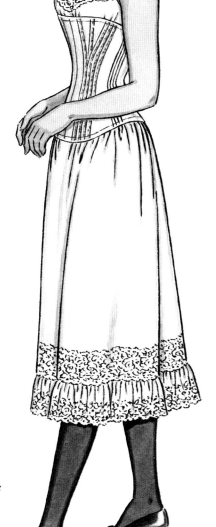

Todd in homemade,
white cotton drawers

Mrs. Dunbar in fine corset of silk satin,
in popular yellow,
with delicate floral-embroidered trim,
over lace-trimmed cotton batiste chemise

Mayetta in white, cotton-cambric corset
cover and petticoat, trimmed in tucks
and narrow lace

From the Journal of Mayetta Spears

March 10, 1889: Today is my sixteenth birthday. Aunt Caroline sent me this journal with the smoothest cover of linen. The Kansas sky has wispy clouds today, and when I went for eggs the wind swirled around the barn and took my bonnet right into the air. Plenty of eggs, but Father says the wheat and corn must do very well this year if we are to stay. After five years of drought and grasshoppers, he says we cannot afford another busted harvest.

Baby Alfred is one month old tomorrow. That makes five of us Spears children. Christine is eleven, young Jed eight. Todd will be eighteen in June; Father says he couldn't manage the farm without him. I only wish Todd liked farming as much as Father does.

April 20, 1889: Todd and Father began breaking the sod early this morning. I tied my bonnet to keep the dust from my eyes and took them bread and sausage at noon. The air was still brisk, but they were hot and thirsty. Charlie, the younger of the two draft horses, was frisky and headstrong. It took both Todd and Father to control the plow behind the horses.

Mrs. Dunbar in Lawrence wrote to me, asking whether I would sew two summer dresses for her. She liked the traveling cape I made for Mrs. Robinson last winter. I am happy my sewing will contribute something to the family!

May 2, 1889: Todd took me in the wagon to visit Mrs. Dunbar in Lawrence today. I wore my good calico into town and borrowed Mother's straw hat with the russet bow. Since my birthday, I have let down my hems and put up my hair. Now I really feel grown up. What a grand house Mrs. Dunbar has! Mr. Dunbar is an official with the Santa Fe Railway, and they travel all over the country, to New York and Chicago and everywhere! I took her measurements for the new dresses. Of course she already had the patterns and the beautiful silks—lilac faille and a delicate stripe—and velvet for the collar and cuffs she'd purchased in Chicago. Also a cool, crisp pink dimity of cotton. What a pleasure it will be to work with such fine fabrics!

May 17, 1889: Oh, what a terrible day! I can hardly write of it. Mother and I were baking bread this morning when Todd rode up to the house hollering like there was a grass fire. Father was caught under the wagon on the south pasture, and Todd could not lift it alone. I galloped bareback on old Chestnut all the way to the Lindhurst's, more than two miles across the prairie. Mr. Lindhurst brought his two sons and with Todd they were able to lift the wagon from Father's legs.

Oh, mercy, the pain Father is in! Mother says we must be thankful he is alive. Doctor Reid came from Lawrence and told mother that if Father's legs begin to darken they must be removed. It is too dreadful to consider.

And to think it was poor Charlie's fault. He spooked when a rabbit dashed out from the grass alongside the road. I suppose we will sell him now, if anyone cares to buy him.

June 8, 1889: It has rained all day today. Todd sat on the porch watching the downpour. I baked with Mother and tended Father's dressings and then sat with Todd. It seems Kansas always has too much of everything: too many grasshoppers, too much sun, too much wind, too much rain.

July 10, 1889: It has not rained since mid-June. The corn and wheat are shriveling under the July sun. It is so hot and humid that Christine and I take baby Alfred and Jed down to the nearly dry creek and stand in the mud to cool off. Christine, Mother, and I tend the cows and the chickens, bake and cook. Todd has so much work trying to tend to the animals and the dying crops both. It seems impossible that this year could be worse than the last few.

July 15, 1889: Yesterday I received a photograph of Mrs. Dunbar in the faille dress I made her. Mr. Dunbar is standing beside her with several other railroad officials and their wives on the Dunbars' wide porch in Lawrence. I wish I could see the lovely lilac of the dress. We are very nearly the same size, and I was able to try on the dress before she came for it. Even so, the world of fancy dresses and luncheons on the grass seems as far away from the Spears farm and all our troubles as the Pacific Ocean.

September 12, 1889: There will be a small harvest this fall, enough, perhaps, to keep the cows and horses through the winter. But nothing to sell. Father told us tonight that we will lose the farm unless Todd finds work in town. The Lindhursts will help Todd bring in the corn and wheat and then Todd will go into Lawrence.

October 17, 1889: Mother, Christine, and I all pitched in to get Todd ready to go to Lawrence to look for work. We altered father's suit and had to do quite a bit of letting out as Todd has grown bigger than father! There was no money for anything new, so of course we had to make do. I must say he looked handsome and grown up, especially with father's watch chain and hat, too.

October 25, 1889: Todd spoke with Mr. Dunbar about work with the railroad. Yesterday, Mr. Dunbar sent a messenger out to the farm with news of work in Topeka with a track gang. Christine and I helped Todd pack a small bag with clothes. I can hardly bear to see him leave.

February 19, 1890: Two friends of Mrs. Dunbar's have asked me to sew dresses for them. Christine is not in school anymore, having finished eighth grade, and we spend most of these cold winter days beside the stove in the front room sewing and talking. Father sits with us, sometimes reading aloud, sometimes silent and pensive. He walks with crutches. I know he is very worried: even with Todd's wages, which have kept us from foreclosure, Father worries about the future of the farm.

March 2, 1890: A letter from Todd today included an advertisement from the Topeka newspaper about work at the Harvey House. It said, "Wanted: women of good character between the ages of 18 and 30, to go west and work for Fred Harvey." Todd wrote that he eats in the Topeka Harvey House every week and knows lots of the girls who are called Harvey Girls. They make $17.50 a month, in addition to room and board! That's almost as much as Todd makes with the track gang. I looked at Mother and Father after reading the letter aloud to everyone. Father shook his head and said decent girls don't work as waitresses in Topeka. Mother reminded me that I'm only sixteen. But I'll be seventeen in eight days, and everyone says I look even older.

April 3, 1890: The bank in Lawrence said we must sell a third of the farm to meet the note. Little Jed missed the last month of school so that he could work with Christine and me preparing the fields. Father came out with us, but cannot walk without the crutches. Christine and I look like farmers now in our old calicos and sunbonnets, our hands all sunburned. We sew in the evenings. Thank goodness for all of Mrs. Dunbar's friends in Lawrence who like our work. I am sewing a silk dress of porcelain blue for Mrs. Dunbar. How beautiful it is, and delicate—Christine and I must handle it with the greatest care!

May 10, 1890: Todd came home today for a visit. Everyone was so excited to see him, it was like Christmas! Even Father laughed and joked. After everyone had gone to bed, Todd and I sat on the porch. Todd said Father will lose all of the farm unless something is done. He said I should come back to Topeka with him and apply for a position as a Harvey Girl. I can hardly fall asleep tonight, thinking about Topeka. But what will Father and Mother say? Do I even want to leave the farm, hard as life is here?

July 12, 1890: How the weeks have flown since I last wrote! I sit in my dormitory room above the Harvey House looking down at Topeka's Holliday Street. A few wagons and riders pass beneath, the summer sky still holding a bit of light. How tired I am! I have not even changed from my starched, stiff uniform. My roommate, Cora, a blacksmith's daughter from Missouri, is down the hall talking with Rose, the head waitress, about a customer who was especially difficult today. Rose is telling Cora what she always tells Harvey Girls: we are here to take good care of all

Harvey House customers, most especially the difficult ones. Remember, Rose says, train travelers are often tired and cranky after sitting for hours on the train.

I do not know what Todd said to Father to convince him to let me return to Topeka with him, but Father and Mother finally agreed I should try for a job with Harvey. I didn't have much to pack in my little bag. Of course I packed this journal. I want to record everything. Mother and Christine were crying when I climbed into the wagon with Todd. I must say I cried, too. Father gave me the Bible that belonged to his mother and then turned back towards the barn—it broke my heart to see how difficult it still seems for him to walk.

I was interviewed by a Miss Clarence in Topeka. Miss Clarence works with the Harvey Company in Kansas City and sometimes interviews applicants in Topeka. I was so nervous that my hands shook and I had to hold them tightly on my lap. I wore the new skirt and shirtwaist I'd made for the trip, but I still looked like a green country girl, right off the farm and all. But Miss Clarence said I spoke very well and had nice manners. I began training the next morning. There was no pay for a month, and I had to agree to obey Harvey's rules about the dormitory and curfew (every girl must live in the Harvey dormitory, which has a ten o'clock curfew. Of course, mother and father are happy about this!); clothes (clean and freshly starched uniforms, no jewelry—except for our numbered uniform pin—makeup, or chewing gum, ever!) and hair (put neatly up). I signed a nine month contract, in which I agreed not to marry (!) until my term was completed. That very day I was placed in a room with Cora, who had been a Harvey Girl for four months. Bertha, an experienced Harvey Girl, was assigned to train me, and I followed her every day for a month.

Everything has to be done in the Harvey way: we keep our station spotless, every chair and table, sugar bowl, salt and pepper shaker cleaned after every meal, the clean linen napkins folded, the silverware polished (and polished and polished). The counter tops and coffee urns gleam! If I spill something on my uniform, I go upstairs and change into a clean one. The cup code took a few days to learn: the way a coffee cup is set on the saucer tells the drink girl if the customer wants tea or coffee or milk. I was nervous and tired the first week, and sometimes went to my room between meals to feel sorry for myself. But all of the other girls say they felt the same, and I really do like my new friends. With a few cranky exceptions, the train passengers are for the most part friendly people. I would never have known the world was so full of interesting people had I not become a Harvey Girl!

And so it all began. Now I am a full-fledged Harvey Girl with blisters on my feet to prove it!

July 30, 1890: Cora and I work the lunch counter three meals a day, six days a week. We have a few hours off between trains, but when the train pulls into the depot and the boy on the platform sounds the gong, it is pandemonium around the Harvey House!

Passenger orders are sent ahead to us by telegraph. Even so, we have to be very fast and organized to serve all of the passengers within the thirty minutes before they must reboard. After the train leaves, just the local people come and work is a little easier, although the railroad men are always making jokes and small talk with the Harvey Girls. It makes me blush, but Cora says they are just being friendly. Many of them are far from home, too.

I've come to know some of the busboys from the community. They live in their own quarters. Harvey Girls are not allowed to date them, but we are all friends. Frank and Erik are brothers from Topeka. They remind me of my own brothers, the way they tease each other and all the Harvey Girls between trains. It really is like a family here at the Harvey House. But I still miss my own on the farm!

August 16, 1890: My day off. I will keep busy with my Christmas sewing. I am making Jed a heavy wool coat for winter. I see the most beautiful clothes on the ladies riding the train in from the East! I sketch and make notes so I won't forget what their dresses look like.

Sometimes I am so homesick I want to lie on my bed and cry. Todd is only in Topeka a few days a week. The other days he is out on the line, sometimes as far away as Newton or Dodge City where he says the rowdiest cowboys in the land come off the trail. When Todd comes to the Harvey House, he always sits at my station. Of course, all the Harvey Girls are mad about him. In his worn work clothes, his face sunburned despite his broad-brimmed hat, he looks so handsome and responsible.

I send most of my pay home to the farm. I have so few needs here in Topeka, even my laundry is taken care of. I did have to buy some sturdy new boots, and black stockings. Cora says to keep some money for our day off when we go down to the five-and-dime. But I don't usually buy anything. Cora likes to get licorice sticks and pretty hair combs. Mother's birthday is next month and I am putting aside some money to buy her some percale at Evans Mercantile. She hasn't had a new dress in so long.

January 5, 1891: I could not go home for Christmas. Neither could Todd, so we celebrated together here in Topeka. Men are not allowed in the women's dormitory above the Harvey House so the Harvey employees—busboys and cooks and kitchen helpers, Harvey Girls, and some railroaders, too—had a party downstairs in the manager's quarters. Mr. Bucknell knew we were all sad about not being home and let us have some of the chef's left-over special holiday desserts. We had chocolate mousse and cherry pie with ice cream! Mother made me a muffler and sent Todd a pair of wool socks. It is so cold out on the line in winter, I don't know how Todd tolerates the wind and blowing snow.

Todd brought a friend to our party, Joshua, another railroader from Illinois. We danced and talked under Mr. and Mrs. Bucknells' watchful eyes.

April 11, 1891: After a visit home to the farm, I renewed my contract for another nine months. It was so good to be home! The fields were just beginning to green, and there were baby chicks and a calf. Father has begun work as a cabinetmaker for people in Lawrence. He will never be able to walk without the canes. With the Lindhurst's help, he plants enough wheat and alfalfa and corn to support the stock and to keep Mother in flour, but nothing more. The Lindhursts are using our other fields. At least we have been able to keep most of the farm.

Father enjoys carpentry. He learned woodwork as a child back in Vermont. He says it brings back good memories of New England. He still wishes I wasn't a waitress. I keep telling him Harvey Girls are *never* called waitresses in Topeka, but I'm not certain he believes me.

September 20, 1891: I went to a dance at the parish hall with Cora and Todd this evening in my new fall dress. I copied it from a traveler. She was from Boston and was on her way to Colorado where her husband owns a silver mine. She was very demure and delicate. I wonder how she will fare in the wild west beyond Topeka. They say "no ladies west of Dodge City; no women west of Albuquerque!"

December 12, 1891: Cora's contract is up, and she has renewed with a request that she be transferred to a Harvey House in New Mexico. Todd was sent to Las Vegas, New Mexico in October. He is studying to be a telegrapher so that he can get out of the cold winter weather along the tracks. I think Cora is going to New Mexico because Todd is there. She has asked me to go, too. New Mexico! Other Harvey people say it is still frontier out there. They say they have bandits and Indians and all kinds of ruffians. Still, I have thoughts about going.

February 18, 1892: Mr. and Mrs. Dunbar came into the Harvey House today. I was so happy to see them I almost cried. Mrs. Dunbar squeezed my hand and told me she missed my sewing. She wore the most exquisite traveling outfit of a stunning blue—her best color. They are on their way to Albuquerque, which Mr. Dunbar says may be a very important city one day. "It's just desert now," Mrs. Dunbar added, laughing.

June 20, 1892: Las Vegas, New Mexico: I rode the train across Kansas—oh, the cattle and dust and smell of Dodge and Newton!—and into Colorado. It was hot and sticky. But that was nothing compared to the ride into the mountains and then up and over Raton Pass! I have never seen such mountains and rocks, pine trees reaching into the clouds, and then far below us valleys of green meadows and wild flowers! How I wish Christine and mother could see this country!

Tonight I am in the Las Vegas Harvey House. Cora and I share a room, and I even know two other Harvey Girls, Olive Strickland and Brenda Klenke, who also came from Topeka. But New Mexico is not Kansas! It is another country! Las Vegas is on the old Santa Fe Trail. There are sheep and cattle ranchers and men with holsters, Indians with long black braided hair and buckskin pants and beautiful moccasins, and it seems everyone but me speaks Spanish. It was on the rooftop of one of the old buildings near the plaza that General Kearny declared U.S. possession of the Territory in 1846. New Town Las Vegas is down here near the tracks; Old Town, up around the plaza.

October 15, 1892: Joshua came through the Harvey House today on his way to Albuquerque where he will be working as an assistant engineer. I was so surprised to see him that I spilled tomato soup on my uniform and had to run upstairs to change. He said he can get train passes and would come up to visit Todd—and me—in the next few months.

November 25, 1892: Thanksgiving at the Harvey House is really very special. Many of the town folks come in, and there is a festive, family atmosphere. Of course, the food is the best in the world. Our chef is from Germany, and he makes everything—even turkey!—something special. I think about Mother and Father, Christine, and Jed and little Alfred back in Kansas. My heart is glad that I have been able to help them keep the farm.

Tonight I sit in my room, Cora already asleep, and look out at the tracks and across the plains, where there is a little snow. Every time the whistle of an incoming train blows I find myself watching to see if Joshua might not get off.

February 10, 1893: Joshua came up from Albuquerque on the late train yesterday. We went ice skating with Todd and Cora up the canyon by Montezuma Castle. It was bitter cold. I wore my warm wool skirt and jacket, but I was still quite frozen. Joshua built a fire, and we sat as close to it as we dared!

Montezuma Castle is a grand Harvey hotel with more than two hundred rooms! It was built in 1882 way up in a remote canyon, six miles outside of Las Vegas, because of the hot springs that are nearby. It is a resort for wealthy travelers from all over the world. In the front lobby, they have a little pool with Mexican turtles, and fresh fruits are brought in year round on the train. (We have fresh fruit at the Harvey House in town, too.) In the winter, covered with snow, the Montezuma looks like something out of a fairy tale.

March 11, 1893: Alicia, one of the Harvey Girls, boarded a train for Arkansas today. Her father, who came to America from Germany to homestead, died of the flu. I think of my own father, working away in his wood shop in the barn on the farm, and thank God he has survived the tragedy that befell him almost four years ago.

Alicia will have a job waiting for her here, if she wants to return. She didn't know when she left whether she would be coming back.

I realize how quickly life can change. I work so terrifically hard in the lunchroom that I can hardly

walk up the stairs to my room each night. And still, I would miss the Harvey House, the other girls, Cora, Todd, Joshua, even the railroaders, if I had to leave and return home to Kansas.

July 27, 1893: What a flurry of activity and excitement today! Fred Harvey himself came to Las Vegas. He came off the train and onto the platform and right into the lunchroom. Everyone knew who he was immediately and scurried to make our service perfect. He spoke with all the girls (even me!) and told us we were doing a fine job. The only complaint I heard was about the orange juice in the cooler. He poured it down the drain and told the cook it had to be freshly squeezed for every meal.

April 22, 1894: Joshua is an engineer now, on the line between Albuquerque and El Paso. I am so disappointed that he was assigned to the southern route. I enjoy his company—we talk and laugh so easily. Now I shall not see him so often.

August 24, 1894: Todd has been transferred to the telegraph office in Albuquerque. Cora has already requested a position at the Harvey House there. It is only a matter of time before she goes.

I am almost twenty-two and feel very much alone. Rose, the head waitress, says she is going to marry and retire by Christmas and that I am in a good position to become head waitress. I don't know: I imagine myself sewing alone in my room, an old maid far from home. There are many single men around the railroad; they come in for lunch every day. But it is Joshua I think about, and he is hundreds of miles to the south.

December 8, 1894: Todd asked Cora to marry him last month. They are planning a June wedding in Missouri. I am to be the maid of honor. Cora will stay in Las Vegas until March when her contract with Harvey is up, and then she will return home. We have been staying up late after work looking through magazines left at the Harvey House by travelers, studying dress and hair styles. I will sew Cora's wedding dress and my bridesmaid dress. We will send away to Kansas City for some of the lovely new figured lawns and lace.

March 10, 1895: My twenty-second birthday. What a birthday it has been! Todd and Joshua came up on the train and surprised Cora and me during the dinner rush. There was a trainload of people demanding food, and we could hardly pause to say hello. After the train left and we had cleaned our stations, we changed out of our uniforms and walked with the boys up to the plaza. There were three Mexican guitarists playing on the steps of the bandstand. It was a beautiful New Mexican night, and we ate bizcochitos—sugar cookies topped with cinnamon—freshly made by an old Spanish woman. We made it back to the dormitory just before our ten o'clock curfew. After Cora and Todd left, Joshua said he had a very special present for me. It was a ring of

(*continued on page* 25)

Mayetta's white cotton sunbonnet

Mother's straw hat
with russet fabric bow

Todd's homemade overalls of
bluish-gray heavy cotton twill,
over gray shirt

Mayetta's plaid gingham
Mother Hubbard

Mayetta's two-piece maize calico dress
with sewing basket

Mrs. Dunbar's dull-red bustle
or dress improver

Todd's made-over suit
of black worsted-wool serge
and black wool felt hat

Mrs. Dunbar's summer dress of lilac silk faille
with striped, soft silk bodice front and skirt; velvet
collar and cuffs; and matching straw hat

Natural straw hat with flower trim

Christine's calico dress with apron

Mrs. Dunbar's porcelain-blue silk visiting dress with floral-embroidered trim and soft white silk bodice front

Mayetta's 1890 Harvey Girl uniform

Navy wool felt hat trimmed
with black satin bow and bird

Mayetta's traveling suit of water-
repellant navy wool with black
braid trim; white percale shirtwaist
with red stripes

Todd's railroad work suit of black
wool with wool muffler and
broad-brimmed wool felt hat

Mayetta's rust satin fall hat
with white plume trim

Mrs. Dunbar's traveling cape
of royal-blue wool serge
with black Baltic seal fur trim

Mrs. Dunbar's traveling suit
of royal-blue wool serge,
trimmed with silk braid;
matching wool felt hat,
with black satin trim and plume

Mayetta's new fall dress of salmon
brocade with rust satin trim
and white chiffon bodice details,
worn to parish hall dance

Black derby hat

Todd's made-over wedding suit
of charcoal gray worsted wool

Cora's wedding dress of aquamarine
flowered cotton lawn with satin collar
and sash; batiste bodice front; and lace
sleeve ruffles, cuffs, and short veil with
satin bow (also to be used as a summer
dress); flower trim matches bouquet

Cora's 1892 Harvey Girl
uniform

Bridesmaid hat of gray straw
with white batiste roses

Cora's black-background, print
chintz maternity wrapper

Mayetta's white-figured
cotton lawn bridesmaid dress
of cool lavender-gray,
with satin trim, batiste yoke
and bodice trim,
and lace ruffles and cuffs

Christine's tan wool jacket trimmed
in beaver fur and tan felt hat
with ribbon trim and plume

Theo's tan felt Rough Rider hat

Theo's Rough Rider uniform:
blue wool shirt and heavy khaki
cotton-twill pants

Christine's champagne silk shirtwaist
with brown velvet ribbon trim and
tan wool skirt

Christine's 1898
head waitress uniform

Theo's thick wool coat

Theo's pale gray felt ranch hat

Christine's holiday dress of
pale lime silk with cream lace

Theo's suit of dark navy-blue
worsted wool serge and black derby

(*continued from page* 6)

silver made by an Indian woman in Albuquerque. An engagement ring! (Of course I said yes!) Since he slipped it on my finger, I can hardly stop gazing at my hand. But there is no time for daydreaming. The next few months will be so busy, finishing Cora's and my dresses for her wedding, and, of course, making over Mr. Dunbar's fine suit for Todd. What a good friend Mr. Dunbar is to insist that Todd have his pick of several suits that no longer fit him but may easily be adjusted for Todd.

From the Journal of Christine Spears

September 13, 1897, Florence, Kansas: For my nineteenth birthday, Mayetta sent me this calico covered journal. She said she has a journal that kept her company all through her years as a Harvey Girl. Now that she is a married woman expecting her first child, I suppose she doesn't have so much time alone. Still, as an engineer, Joshua is often gone on what they call the Horny Toad line between Albuquerque and El Paso.

Here at the Clifton, the finest hotel in Kansas, we serve three meal trains a day with fifty people per meal! We serve the passengers family style, ten people to a table. The local community can eat at the counter, where lunch is less expensive than in the dining room. We also have rainwater baths that anyone can take for twenty-five cents. The most elegant women I have ever seen stay overnight in Florence. I must send some sketches of their fashions to Mayetta.

November 11, 1897: I have asked for a position in New Mexico when I renew my contract in December. Mr. Barker, our manager, says I have a good chance of going to Las Vegas or Albuquerque. Mayetta and Joshua are in Albuquerque; Todd and Cora have moved back to Las Vegas.

February 19, 1898: Las Vegas, New Mexico: There may be plenty of desert in New Mexico, but here on the edge of the Sangre de Cristo mountains it is bitter cold. We had several feet of snow yesterday, and a train was stranded on the north side of Raton Pass for several hours. When the passengers finally came into the Harvey House, they were cold, exhausted, hungry, and ill-tempered. But our hot coffee, fresh bread and thick slices of roast beef lulled even the most difficult customer into a better frame of mind.

April 15, 1898: Todd and Cora have a little adobe house up near the Old Town plaza, and I often go there on my day off to sew and talk with Cora.

Mayetta had a baby girl last month: she named her Lorraine for our mother. I only wish Mother and Father could come to New Mexico and visit us all!

Cora is expecting a child in October, so we are making maternity wrappers for her. Father made Cora and Todd an oak pedestal table with extra leaves. It arrived on the train several weeks ago. We cut our patterns on its long smooth top.

November 10, 1898: Last month Cora had a baby boy—Allan—and I became head waitress. Marcella, the former head waitress, had to return to Kentucky because her mother is ill. I have the most seniority, so, even though I'm only twenty, I was promoted. I have new uniforms: while the other Harvey Girls wear black blouses and skirts with a white apron, I wear a black skirt with a white blouse, and a handsome black tie. I no longer share a room and am enjoying the space for my sewing machine. I am helping to break in three new Harvey Girls who arrived from Kansas yesterday. They are all homesick, and looked so relieved that the head waitress was a Kansas farmer's daughter!

The Santa Fe is building a new brick Harvey House along the tracks. It will be called the Castañeda and will be two stories high with thirty guest rooms! They will close down our little Harvey House, and everyone will move into the elegant new hotel next spring. Imagine! I will be living in one of the finest hotels in the West!

June 4, 1899: We have moved into the new Castañeda. It is a beautiful place to live. The furniture in the guest rooms, and in the dining and lunch rooms, was all made specially for the hotel. All of the local customers have been flocking in to enjoy a meal in the new lunchroom, and the train passengers are simply overwhelmed by the atmosphere when they step off the train. "Way out here in the Territory of New Mexico," one Chicago woman said, "who would have believed it?"

June 10, 1899: We are preparing for a large celebration for Governor Roosevelt's Rough Riders later this month. The men of the First United States Volunteer Cavalry, who rode together in the Spanish-American War, will have a reunion here in Las Vegas. It is rumored that Governor Roosevelt, the cavalry's leader, will be staying here in the Castañeda.

June 15, 1899: What a hectic two days it has been! Very nearly every person in the community of Las Vegas came to the depot to meet Theodore Roosevelt's train yesterday. Mr. Bennett, the manager, says he heard there were five thousand people along the tracks and around the hotel! The Rough Riders all came in their uniforms, many of them local rancher's sons. Some of Roosevelt's Indian friends came. There were many speeches and a band played almost all afternoon. The Castañeda porches were so crowded with people that when the supper train came in, we had to use all the busboys to guide the passengers from the train into the dining room and back out again before the train left. It was all very exciting and exhausting—I had to keep all the girls on their toes and away from the activity outside. Sometimes I believe it is easier to be just a Harvey Girl and not the head waitress.

June 16, 1899: Roosevelt is staying here in the hotel, but his men are in tents outside of town. I wandered over to the Old Town plaza this afternoon with some other Harvey Girls. One of the soldiers came over and asked me where I was from. His name is Theodore, just like the Governor's! Although he's not an officer, he still looked very dashing in his regulation trousers and shirt (they must be unbearably hot in this climate this time of year). Theo was raised on a ranch near Wagon Mound, a town near the old Santa Fe trail. He rarely comes into Las Vegas, although he said he'd always heard the Harvey House had lots of pretty girls. Now, he said, he would believe those stories!

December 20, 1899: The new century is almost upon us. The Castañeda looks so lovely covered with snow and decorated with piñon branch wreaths and red ribbons. I feel pretty festive myself, now that my new holiday silk is finished. When I gaze east out the windows of my own room onto the beautiful wintry plains, I am filled with the Christmas spirit. Joshua and Mayetta have asked me to come to Albuquerque for Christmas. Todd and Cora invited me to spend the holiday with them if I stay in Las Vegas. Theo says his family has a big Christmas on the ranch, but if it doesn't snow too hard, he will come into town to visit me. I guess I will stay in Las Vegas. Besides, I'd rather be where Theo could find me if he is able to leave the ranch. I will pray for clear weather.

December 26, 1899: It has snowed without stopping for three days now. When I am not working downstairs in the dining room, I have been sitting in my room watching the snow on the plains and sewing. Of course Theo will not ride through such a blizzard. It would be dangerous.

I sent mother and father a large box of presents on the train. Father's carpentry business is doing fine, but Mother still won't spend much money on frivolities for herself or Jed and Alfred. Theo told me about the horn-handled knives an Indian friend makes and helped me pick one for Father. For months Cora and I admired the blankets a local Spanish woman makes with the wool from her sheep. Together we bought one for Mother. I sent Jed and Al sheepskin hats like the ones the northern New Mexico mountain men wear.

New Year's Eve, 1899: Theo rode up to the hotel before dusk. Under his ranch hat and thick wool coat, he was warm enough, but his moustache was all icicles. It was a long ride, longer than usual because of drifts over the road.

We went in all our finery to the New Year's Eve party for the Harvey employees and then sat bundled in blankets on the Castañeda porch. Theo said there is simply too much distance between his place and mine and would I mind terribly marrying him and moving to the ranch? He has plans for his own ranch and has been eyeing a section of land a couple of miles from his father's to homestead and raise cattle.

We will be married in the late spring here in New Mexico. I will send Mother and Father, little Alfred and Jed train tickets, and they will see New Mexico at last! Maybe we can even convince them to stay!